101 REASONS WHY YOU'RE BETTER OFF SINGLE

MICHAEL O'MARA BOOKS LIMITED

First published in Great Britain in 2006 by
Michael O'Mara Books Limited
9 Lion Yard, Tremadoc Road
London SW4 7NQ

A CIP catalogue record for this book is available
from the British Library

ISBN (10 digit): 1-84317-195-3
ISBN (13 digit): 978-1-84317-195-9

1 3 5 7 9 10 8 6 4 2

www.mombooks.com

Designed and typeset by Martin Bristow

Printed and bound in Great Britain
by William Clowes Ltd, Beccles, Suffolk

Introduction

Whether you've just split up from your husband or boyfriend, or simply grown tired of the seemingly fruitless hunt for the man of your dreams, *101 Reasons Why You're Better Off Single* will provide heartfelt, rock-solid and often amusing assurances that singledom is a status to be treasured.

Think about it: how many of life's irritating moments are directly related to the unfathomable behaviour of our so-called 'life partners'? And how much happier would our lives be *without* them?

Imagine the following blissful scenarios: *not* having to organize your life around anyone else; relaxing in front of the TV in sole command of the remote control; *never* having to watch an episode of *Top Gear* again; *not* being taken for granted where the cooking and cleaning are concerned; being spared the ritual of putting the toilet seat back in its rightful place at *every* visit . . . Embracing the single life guarantees all of the above ideals, and much more besides.

Offering a wake-up call to anyone in a relationship long past its sell-by date, *101 Reasons Why You're Better Off Single* proves beyond all doubt why the grass is always greener when you're single.

Dressed to Kill

#1

You can practically live at your local salon
without being told by your other half
that you spend more time with your
hairdresser than you do with him.
It's not as if he ever noticed the
result anyway . . .

#2

Without a partner to please,
you're no longer obliged to don
a cheese-slicer thong or scratchy lace
g-string on a daily basis. In fact,
you could consign to the scrapheap
all the dodgy underwear you've ever
been bought. Better still, burn it.

You have two choices in life:
You can stay single and be miserable,
or get married and wish you were dead.
AUTHOR UNKNOWN

#3

If you don't feel like enduring agonizing pain for the sake of looking good on your partner's arm, in the single girl's world there's no longer any reason to wear ridiculously high heels on a night out.

> *Sometimes I think if there was a third sex men wouldn't get so much as a glance from me.*
> AMANDA VAIL

#4

When you wake up in the morning
with your hair like a bird's nest,
your face sporting a shiny new spot
and your breath pungent enough
to stun a skunk, it's a blessed relief
to realize there's nobody lying next
to you to witness you at your worst.

#5

If you feel like having some fun on a no-strings-attached basis, you can plan a different date for every night of the week. Be wined and dined, go dancing till the wee small hours, and be swept off your feet knowing that you'll be seeing someone new the next evening!

6

After a hard day's work, if you fancy
lounging about the house in a baggy
tracksuit, dressing gown or an old pair
of pyjamas, you can do so without
worrying whether your other half
will ever want to sleep with you again.

★ ★ ★

*❛I'm single
because I was born that way.❜*
MAE WEST

#7

When you're out on the town,
you don't have to be uncomfortably
clad in stockings, suspenders or a sexily
unsupportive bra just to indulge
a boyfriend or husband.
Instead you can dress
to please yourself.

★ ★ ★

*❝Marriage is a bargain,
and somebody has to get the worst
of the bargain.❞*
HELEN ROWLAND

#8

No more guilty secret pampering –
as a single girl, appointments
with beauty therapists for regular
nail and facial treatments can be made
openly and with pride. So get those
nails buffed and blitz those wrinkles!

9

When you're trying to look your best for a big night out, you can take as much time as you need when there's no one breathing down your neck. A single girl doesn't have to endure impatient shouts of 'Are you nearly ready?' while getting glammed up for a night on the town.

Fun Indoors

#10

There's nobody to challenge your supreme control over the TV remote control – complete command of this valued tool now lies squarely in your hands. Flicking channels isn't half so irritating when it's you doing the flicking.

If I ever marry, it will be on a sudden impulse – as a man shoots himself.
H. L. MENCKEN

#11

You can spend hours on the phone
to your best friend/mum/other men
without having to block out the series
of tuts and dramatic sighs from the
idiot on the sofa.

#12

The sky's the limit as far as pets
are concerned – you can breed llamas,
farm ostriches, keep komodo dragons
or merely adopt a kitten when you're
enjoying the single life. The choice
is yours, and no one else's.

#13

You can stay in bed all weekend reading
trashy novels from cover to cover or
watching black-and-white films from the
depths of the duvet, just because you
feel like it.

*❛My husband and I divorced over religious
differences. He thought he was God,
and I didn't.❜*

AUTHOR UNKNOWN

#14

Gone are the days where you have
to pretend to appreciate (or even
understand) the offside rule, baseball
or American football. You can bask
in ignorance of such matters for the rest
of your life without fear of recrimination.

*‘I never knew what real happiness
was until I got married.
And by then it was too late.’*
MAX KAUFFMAN

#15

None of your highly original hobbies,
such as macramé, tatting, bee-keeping
or deep-sea diving, will ever be mocked
with such patronizing contempt again.

#16

If sport isn't your cup of tea, the single
life ensures that you will never have
to endure a single second of World Cup
action (whether it be football, cricket
or rugby), Formula One motor racing,
the Olympics (summer or winter),
horse racing or golf ever again.

#17

Programmes about cars, monster trucks,
DIY and war can be officially banned
from your television screen, now that
you're solely responsible for paying
the licence fee.

*Sometimes I wonder if men and women
really suit each other. Perhaps they
should live next door and just visit
now and then.*
KATHARINE HEPBURN

#18

You're no longer obliged to feign interest
in bloodthirsty war films, scary sci-fi
movies, crazy cult 'classics',
or pretentious art-house productions
of dubious merit, and instead are free
to indulge your deeply held love
of chick flicks.

*A wedding is just like a funeral
except that you get to smell
your own flowers.*
GRACE HANSEN

#19

The only diary you have to consult
before arranging a night out is your own
– fitting in your socializing around
an annoyingly inflexible partner
is no longer an issue.

#20

From Abba to Steps, Britney to
Black Lace, you're free to play your
eclectic range of music at full blast
to your heart's content and no one
will bat an eyelid . . . except
perhaps the neighbours.

#21

You can invite all your friends round
for a giggly girly games night whenever
you want, without having to conduct
delicate negotiations with your partner
to get rid of him for the evening.

*⁶Bigamy is having one husband
or wife too many.
Monogamy is the same.⁹*
OSCAR WILDE

#22

You can watch reality TV at any time
of the day or night, and there'll be no
one around to tell you how sad you are.

*Three rings of marriage are the
engagement ring, the wedding ring,
and the suffering.*

AUTHOR UNKNOWN

#23

You can sing wildly off-key and dance
like a maniac in the privacy of your own
home, knowing that your performances
will no longer be subjected to brutally
insensitive criticism by the one-man
audience in the corner.

#24

Unless you throw a party or invite
friends round, all the wine that
you'll ever buy will be guzzled
by you and you alone.

#25

You can cry at your favourite weepie
movie without being laughed at
by an unemotional, unfeeling man
with a heart of stone.

'All marriages are happy.
It's the living together afterward
that causes all the trouble.'
RAYMOND HULL

#26

You won't have to protect your precious takeaways again from the thieving grasp of an eternally over-hungry boyfriend.

'It destroys one's nerves to be amiable every day to the same human being.'
BENJAMIN DISRAELI

#27

Living the single life ensures you can
watch all of *Four Weddings and a Funeral*,
Titanic or *Pretty Woman* without being told
to fast-forward to the sex/action scenes.

#28

As a single girl with no one to please but yourself, you'll never again be forced into playing Xbox or PlayStation games alongside an over-enthusiastic partner. Nor will you have to waste valuable time watching him in action, feigning delight at his extraordinary alien-bashing talents.

Household
Habits

#29

Petty arguments about whose turn
it is to take the rubbish out are
no longer an issue when you're single.
OK, so it's always your turn,
but there's not half so much rubbish
in the first place when your bin
isn't filled with takeaway pizza boxes
and empty beer cans.

30

Without a man around the house to clean up after, you'll no longer be obliged to collect deposits of black stubbly whiskers from the bathroom basin, gather up monstrous piles of toenail clippings from under the bedside lamp or waste precious time extracting hairs from the bathroom soap.

I believe in the single standard for men and women.
MAE WEST

31

Ironing becomes a more manageable
chore without a mile-high pile of men's
shirts to tackle every Sunday night –
which of course must be handled with
the utmost care and attention . . .

Wedding rings:
the world's smallest handcuffs.
AUTHOR UNKNOWN

32

The toilet seat will always stay exactly as you left it. And cleaning the loo is nowhere near such a grim job if there isn't a man around to leave any lingering reminders at the bottom of the bowl.

#33

Living alone as a singleton,
you'll be guaranteed to save
a fortune in industrial-strength
air freshener (read into this
what you will).

#34

Washing up can be saved up over a
period of days – not because you're too
lazy to do it every day, of course,
but to save on hot water – and there'll
be no one else around to criticize.

*⁶What a lovely surprise to finally discover
how unlonely being alone can be.⁹*
ELLEN BURSTYN

#35

In the home of a single girl, wet towels
are never flung on the bathroom floor
in a festering heap, but are always hung
up to dry immediately after use.

*Don't accept rides from strange men,
and remember that all men are strange.*
ROBIN MORGAN

36

The only underwear you'll have to wash
and dry is your own. No more will you
have to touch – ugh! – those crusty pairs
of boxer shorts, briefs or yellowing
Y-fronts that have been decaying for
days in the bottom of the laundry bin
(if you're lucky; on the floor if
you're not . . .).

#37

The pressure to be a domestic goddess
will be lifted without a partner to witness
you struggling with newfangled recipes
for roast dinners, cakes and sauces.
With just yourself to please, life in
the kitchen becomes a breeze.

38

Without a man about the house,
you won't keep finding sweaty socks
down the back of the sofa, nor will you
have to crunch your way over week-old
dirty boxer shorts en route to your bed.
You can even rediscover the pleasure
of walking about your home barefoot,
safe in the knowledge that you won't
tread in anything nasty.

★ ★ ★

Wedlock is a padlock.
JOHN RAY

39

Living the single life means you only
have to clean the bath, dust shelves
or change the bed linen when you're
expecting visitors. Alternatively, if you
like your house just so, you can keep it
that way without some clod-hopping
bloke wandering around, messing it up.

★ ★ ★

*I've sometimes thought of marrying,
and then I've thought again.*
NOËL COWARD

#40

No longer will you be the object of a partner's irrational wrath when he finds that his football kit hasn't been washed or ironed in time for his next game, despite the fact that *he* was the one who left it to rot in the bottom of his sports bag for a week.

41

There are far fewer arguments about household chores when one lives alone in blissful solitude. There's no nagging, no extra mess to clear up and much more free time to devote to pursuits of the non-cleaning variety, i.e. watching TV, eating chocolate and drinking wine.

In the
Bedroom

42

Living the single life ensures you
can make the most of the luxury
of having a whole double bed to yourself.
If you want to sleep like a starfish,
go for it!

43

Eating toast in bed can be done
at leisure, without fear of recrimination.
All crumb patterns, jam splodges or
butter drips are yours and yours alone.

★ ★ ★

The desire to get married, which –
I regret to say, I believe is basic and
primal in women – is followed almost
immediately by an equally basic and
primal urge – which is to be
single again.
NORA EPHRON

44

As a single girl you'll never again be compelled to wrestle with your bedmate for nothing more exciting than a share of the duvet.

❝Marriage is a great institution, but I'm not ready for an institution.❞
MAE WEST

45

Men. Beer. Farts.
Need we say more?

46

You can get up in the middle of the night
and make a doorstep chip butty oozing
with ketchup without having to give a
reason, or make one for anyone else.

'Never marry for money.
Ye'll borrow it cheaper.'
SCOTTISH PROVERB

#47

All the clothes that might be strewn
artistically across the bedroom floor are
yours and yours alone. You can choose
to tidy them up, or you can leave
them there until the time is right
for an invigorating spring clean . . .
whenever that might be.

★ ★ ★

❛I think, therefore I'm single.❜
LIZZ WINSTEAD

#48

No more need for sudden headaches
or faked orgasms now that sex is less
of a routine chore and more an
eagerly anticipated thrill.

By the time you say you're his,
Shivering and sighing,
And he vows his passion is
Infinite, undying —
Lady, make a note of this:
One of you is lying.
DOROTHY PARKER

#49

As a single girl you'll be spared being
roused from your sleep by a cacophony
of snoring produced by the half-drunk
hairy monster by your side.
Of course you might snore yourself –
but *you* don't have to hear it!

50

Who needs a man anyway when you can buy a 'Rampant Rabbit'? It's efficient, reliable, and it doesn't talk back, snore or fart – a perfect combination.

> *The poor wish to be rich,*
> *the rich wish to be happy,*
> *the single wish to be married,*
> *and the married wish to be dead.*
> ANN LANDERS

Shop Till You Drop

51

During single-girl shopping sprees,
you can buy as many scented candles
and joss sticks as you can manage
to stagger home with, and there'll be
no one there to make a fuss about either
the cost or the potential fire hazard.

52

You don't have to explain that regrettably
expensive impulse buy to anyone –
no one need ever know.

*'Any intelligent woman
who reads the marriage contract,
and then goes into it,
deserves all the consequences.'*
ISADORA DUNCAN

53

As a single girl, there's no chance
of being told by an incredulous
boyfriend/husband that adding to
your collection of 100-plus handbags
with matching shoes is in any
way excessive.

*Though marriage makes man and wife
one flesh, it leaves 'em still two fools.*
WILLIAM CONGREVE

54

When you're single, there's no one
around to think you've gone mad
when you get up at 5 a.m. to start
queueing for the first of the
season's sales.

55

In the run-up to Christmas, the only
presents you need to worry about
are those for your own loved ones.
Never again will you be coerced
into buying gifts for his family or friends,
just because he can't be bothered
and you end up feeling guilty (why?!).

56

You don't have to explain the fact
that although you already have sixteen
different lipsticks in your full-to-bursting
make-up bag, it's still essential that
you make regular pilgrimages to every
high-street cosmetics counter to try on
the new shades.

*Men are from Mars,
women are from Venus.*
JOHN GRAY

#57

During expeditions to the supermarket,
you can spend as much time as you
need studying lists of ingredients
and checking the calorific content
of every single item, without being
subjected to a barrage of tuts and
moans from a bored partner.

*‘Marriage is not a word –
it's a sentence.’*
AUTHOR UNKNOWN

#58

So you visit every shoe shop on the
high street, try on a hundred pairs
of heels and then go back to the
original pair in the original shop?
So what!

59

When you're *sans* partner, shopping
becomes a pleasure instead of a pain.
You're free to step across the theshold
of whichever shop takes your fancy,
stress levels are drastically cut,
and peace reigns supreme.
The only problem is, there's no one
to carry all your bags for you . . .

Personal Habits

#60

If you're single, you only have to deal with your own squalid habits (which, because they're yours, may be considered sweet and endearing).

If you want to sacrifice the admiration of many men for the criticism of one, go ahead, get married.
KATHARINE HEPBURN

#61

You can spend an unlimited amount
of guilt-free time in the bath,
and there'll be no one around
to bang on the door shouting,
'Are you finished yet?'

#62

The bathroom is always free,
and thanks to all your lovely sprays,
soaps and scented candles,
it *never* smells bad.

#63

You can pluck your eyebrows,
shave your legs or wax your bikini line
in the comfort of your bedroom,
instead of having to lock yourself
away in the bathroom.

*The chief reason why marriage is
rarely a success is that it is contracted
while the partners are insane.*
JOSEPH COLLINS

#64

A single person living alone never
has to put up with other people's
annoying habits, such as teeth-grinding,
knuckle-cracking and nose-picking.

*The secret of a happy marriage
remains a secret.*
HENNY YOUNGMAN

#65

With no one around to recoil
in disgust, toenails can be clipped
in the comfort of your living room.

#66

You can make yourself look effortlessly
elegant without anyone knowing that,
in reality, it took you five hours of hard
graft to reach your peak of readiness
for the evening ahead.

*Never say that marriage
has more of joy than pain.*
EURIPIDES

#67

Life as a single person means
you don't have to make excuses
or apologize for the odd bout of PMT –
if you want to smash a cup or scream
the place down or just have a
mini-breakdown, you can!

#68

If you decide not to bother showering
for a couple of days, there's no one
around either to notice or to complain.

> *Marriage means commitment.
> Of course, so does insanity.*
> AUTHOR UNKNOWN

Out
and About

69

You can party whenever and wherever
you like, and appreciate every
admiring look, compliment, drink
and date that comes your way.

#70

You can choose to watch cheesy romantic
comedies on Sunday afternoons at
the cinema without any argument.
And the popcorn is all yours.

*‘Why get married and make one man
miserable when I can stay single
and make thousands miserable?’*
CARRIE P. SNOW

71

The only boring work dos you have to attend are your own. Never again will you have to engage in banal small talk, while remaining sensibly but boringly sober, just to avoid embarrassing your husband/boyfriend/partner in front of his colleagues.

★ ★ ★

 The happiest of all lives is a busy solitude.
VOLTAIRE

#72

If you find yourself lost in a strange town, you can just wind down the car window and ask a passing local to point you in the right direction. Simple, huh? Men, of course, would rather insist on driving around aimlessly for three hours in an increasing rage before contemplating this rather more sensible option.

73

Being single saves you the dubious
pleasure of having to support your
boyfriend/husband from the touchline
every other weekend when he's engaged
in Sunday League football or rugby
(or even both, if you're really unlucky).

#74

Every night out can be a girls' night out
when you're unattached, footloose
and fancy-free, and very much up
for a bit of light flirting.

*If you are single there is always one thing
you should take out with you on a Saturday
night . . . your friends.*
SARAH JESSICA PARKER

#75

As a singleton, you won't have to
put up with being annoyed by an errant
partner who can't stop eyeing up other
women while you're out on the town
together, no matter how drop-dead
gorgeous you look yourself.

It's a

Wonderful

Life

76

No more need to be subjected
to patronizing remarks by a partner
on subjects as wide-ranging as cars,
computers, gadgets and DIY – you can
sensibly seek the help of clever experts,
not tiresome amateurs, instead.

#77

You can decorate the house using whichever garish colour schemes you fancy. Minimalism is well and truly out; hot pink, sunset orange and kitschy knick-knacks galore are definitely in.

There's only one way to have a happy marriage and as soon as I learn what it is I'll get married again.

CLINT EASTWOOD

#78

It's easier to get the painting, gardening or DIY jobs done without the procrastinations of an idle partner ringing in your ear. Employing a capable male professional guarantees that the work is done without a fuss; fewer things go wrong; and if you're lucky, he might turn out to be an Adonis in overalls!

❝ [Being single] is pretty good. It's a nice sense of irresponsibility. ❞
MICHAEL DOUGLAS

#79

Single girls never have to feign surprise
or delight when presented with
sub-standard gifts from boyfriends
or husbands lacking the imagination
to buy anything other than garage
flowers, slutty underwear
or cheap boxes of chocolates.

#80

There is no one to subject you to the same inane or tasteless jokes over and over again – why do so many men think that the more often you repeat a joke, the funnier it gets, even if you didn't laugh the first time?

★ ★ ★

The surest way to be alone is to get married.
GLORIA STEINEM

81

As a singleton, you don't have to suffer
the burden of in-laws, whether it be
either the official or unofficial variety.
So never again will you have to force
a fixed smile when your partner's mother
criticizes the meal you've been slaving
over for hours.

*❛Love – a temporary insanity
curable by marriage.❜*
AMBROSE BIERCE

82

You can spend Christmas in the loving embrace of your own family, rather than trying to adapt to the strange customs of your other half's relatives (like having to fend off his slobbery Uncle Stan under the mistletoe).

83

Living the single life means filling up every available inch of space with your own clutter. It does not include making room for a partner's model train set, personal fitness equipment or extensive record collection.

> *Assumptions are the termites of relationships.*
> HENRY WINKLER

#84

Though attending functions (such as weddings) can be daunting as a single girl, it's better than dragging along an unwilling partner by the scruff of his neck. Life as a singleton also avoids the hassle of making credible excuses to cover a partner's guilty absence.

If you are afraid of loneliness, don't marry.

ANTON CHEKHOV

#85

You're no longer obliged to have to have a well-stocked fridge without a partner to cook hearty meals for. Who cares if all your fridge contains is a few cans of cola, bars of chocolate, bottles of wine and sticky buns?

6 My wife and I tried to breakfast together, but we had to stop or our marriage would have been wrecked.9

SIR WINSTON CHURCHILL

86

When you're not living with a human
dustbin, you can guarantee that there's
always some milk left in the fridge,
bread doesn't mysteriously disappear
and the iced bun you've been saving
for Friday night will still be there
two days later.

*Boys will be boys,
and so will a lot of middle-aged men.*
KIN HUBBARD

#87

'Man Flu' is a phenomenon that you never need witness at close hand again. The moans, groans and sorrowful cries of pain will be but a distant memory, as will the tiring experience of nursing a partner who's suffering from nothing more than a sniffle and a tickle in the throat.

88

Being home alone gives you licence
to invite your sexy next-door neighbour
to come round and chase away
scary spiders.

89

You'll never be subjected to comparison
with a partner's saintly mother or
semi-perfect ex-girlfriend (which begs
the question, why is she his ex?).

*❝ I never married because there was
no need. I have three pets at home which
answer the same purpose as a husband.
I have a dog which growls every morning,
a parrot which swears all afternoon,
and a cat that comes home late at night.❞*
MARIE CORELLI

#90

When you're single, you never have
to pretend to fancy your best friend,
or reveal to your partner which of
your friends you'd snog if your life
depended on it.

*The only time a woman really succeeds
in changing a man is when he is a baby.*
NATALIE WOOD

#91

After a rubbish day at work you won't have to come home to an unsympathetic partner, who doesn't take his eyes off the telly while you're pouring out your woes, and only offers you boring practical suggestions rather than giving you the sympathy you desperately need.

❛When a girl marries she exchanges the attentions of many men for the inattention of one.❜

HELEN ROWLAND

92

If you want to spend an hour cooking something delicious, you can savour it yourself with a glass of red and enjoy every mouthful, instead of watching in dismay while your partner gobbles it down in two minutes flat, burps and washes it down with a can of cheap lager.

*❝ I like being single.
I'm always there when I need me.❞*
ART LEO

93

In your single-woman household,
the *Daily/Sunday Sport* will be banned
from crossing your threshold for
evermore, as well as all motoring,
computer and gaming magazines.

#94

Christmas parties are generally more fun
if you are single, allowing you to step
up the flirtation levels without fear
of being found out. It also means
you don't have to drag round your
partner and hope that he doesn't
make a fool of himself (and you).

#95

Without a man about the house
you can avoid having to pay out
expensive subscriptions for
digital/satellite sports channels,
and instead use the money to treat
yourself to a whole library of
black-and-white weepie DVDs.

*Thus Dante's motto over Inferno
applies with equal force to marriage:
"Ye who enter here leave all hope behind."*
EMMA GOLDMAN

96

When it comes to hiring someone
for those difficult-to-do jobs, you can
employ a gardener based purely on
the shape of his bum rather than
his horticultural knowledge.

*Spouse: someone who'll stand by you
through all the trouble you wouldn't have
had if you'd stayed single.*

AUTHOR UNKNOWN

#97

Without a partner in tow, you'll be
spared endless questions from
interfering relatives on the
less-than-thrilling subjects
of marriage and babies.

98

Nothing beats the feeling of being
in control of your own life.
Yes, you can put up shelves
and change a fuse – and you'll
feel brilliant for doing it yourself.

99

Never again will you have to hear the words, 'Haven't you eaten enough?' And diets too can become a thing of the past if you only dieted to please the man in your life.

❝ "I am" is reportedly the shortest sentence in the English language. Could it be that "I do" is the longest sentence? ❞

AUTHOR UNKNOWN

#100

As a fully fledged single person, you are free to decide what *you* want to do when *you* want to do it. There's no more checking with 'im indoors about whether he'll mind if you go out and see your friends every once in a while!

'An object in possession seldom retains the same charm that it had in pursuit.'
PLINY THE YOUNGER

#101

Criticism about your cooking, your size, your appearance and your outgoings will become a thing of the past as a single girl – compliments, reassurances and admiring glances are all that will be coming your way from your ever-reliable source of good and true friends.

Things
You Don't
Have To Hear
If You're Single

Things You Don't Have to Hear If You're Single

'Love, while you're up,
could you get me another beer?'

★ ★ ★

'Go on, have a whiff of that –
it's one of my best!'

★ ★ ★

'No, I'm *not* having an affair
with my secretary.'

★ ★ ★

'Why don't you give
Weight Watchers a go?'

Things You Don't Have to Hear If You're Single

'That vindaloo's made me feel really horny – let's have an early night!'

'It's the World Cup, sweetheart – I can't miss a single match.'

'You'd look like a supermodel too if you ate less chocolate.'

'Yes, your bum *does* look big in that.'

'Let's stay in tonight
and have some fun . . .
on the PlayStation.'

★ ★ ★

'You don't mind another golfing
holiday this year, do you?'

★ ★ ★

'I promise I'll do the painting
and decorating soon . . .'

★ ★ ★

'Don't you worry – *I'll* make dinner.
Beans on toast OK?'

Things You Don't Have to Say If You're Single

Things You Don't Have to Say If You're Single

❝Never mind, darling. Let's try again tomorrow when you're not so tired.❞

❝Of course, you can invite your mother over for Christmas . . . and New Year.❞

❝Oh, those PVC crotchless knickers are for me? Honey, you shouldn't have!❞

❝I'd really love to, sweetie, but I've got such a headache tonight . . .❞

Things You Don't Have to Say If You're Single

❝No problem, love. I'd be happy to wash and iron your filthy, stinking rugby kit.❞

❝Will you PLEASE remember to put the loo seat down when you've finished?❞

❝Can you try it with more haste, less speed next time?❞

❝Please don't get drunk at my office party this year.❞

Things You Don't Have to Say If You're Single

❝No, I'm delighted that you've invited
your fourteen rugby mates round
for a beer, curry and poker night . . .❞

★ ★ ★

❝Of course I like your mother . . .❞

★ ★ ★

❝No, I'd love to join you
for your James Bond film night.❞

★ ★ ★

❝No, I don't mind staying in
while you go out and get plastered
with your friends.❞

Things You Don't Have to Say If You're Single

❛I wish you'd remember
to use the air freshener . . .❜

★ ★ ★

❛Actually, our anniversary
was last month.❜

★ ★ ★

❛Next time you come home drunk
at three in the morning, make sure
you've got your keys.❜

All Michael O'Mara titles are available by post from:

Bookpost, PO Box 29,
Douglas, Isle of Man. IM99 1BQ
Telephone: 01624 677237/Fax: 01624 670923
Email: bookshop@enterprise.net
Internet: www.bookpost.co.uk
Credit cards accepted.
Free postage and packing in the UK.

———————

NEW, EXPANDED 128-PAGE EDITIONS, 95 × 85mm

The Little Book of Stupid Men £2.50
ISBN (10 digit) 1-85479-454-X
ISBN (13 digit) 978-1-85479-454-3

The Little Book of Speed Dating £2.50
ISBN (10 digit) 1-84317-074-4
ISBN (13 digit) 978-1-84317-074-7

The Little Book of Dirty Speed Dating £2.50
ISBN (10 digit) 1-84317-080-9
ISBN (13 digit) 978-1-84317-080-8

The Little Book of Crap Excuses £2.50
ISBN (10 digit) 1-84317-040-x
ISBN (13 digit) 978-1-84317-040-2

The Little Book of Crap Advice £2.50
ISBN (10 digit) 1-84317-041-8
ISBN (13 digit) 978-1-84317-041-9

WAN2TLK? ltle bk of txt msgs £2.50
ISBN (10 digit) 1-84317-082-5
ISBN (13 digit) 978-1-84317-082-2

Dirty Cockney Rhyming Slang £2.50
ISBN (10 digit) 1-84317-035-3
ISBN (13 digit) 978-1-84317-035-8

The Little Book of Internet Dating £2.50
ISBN (10 digit) 1-84317-173-2
ISBN (13 digit) 978-1-84317-173-7

The Little Book of Sex Dares £2.50
ISBN (10 digit) 1-84317-194-5
ISBN (13 digit) 978-1-84317-194-2

ORIGINAL 96-PAGE EDITIONS, 95 × 85mm

The Little Book of Tantric Sex for Busy People £1.99
ISBN (10 digit) 1-85479-685-2
ISBN (13 digit) 978-1-85479-685-1

The Little Book of Sex Fantasies £1.99
ISBN (10 digit) 1-85479-725-5
ISBN (13 digit) 978-1-85479-725-4

72-PAGE CHEQUE BOOKS, 70 × 200mm

Sex Cheques £3.50
ISBN (10 digit) 1-84317-121-X
ISBN (13 digit) 978-1-84317-121-8

Sex Maniac's Cheques £2.99
ISBN (10 digit) 1-85479-434-5
ISBN (13 digit) 978-1-85479-434-5

Hot Sex Cheques £3.50
ISBN (10 digit) 1-84317-069-8
ISBN (13 digit) 978-1-84317-069-3